I0819438

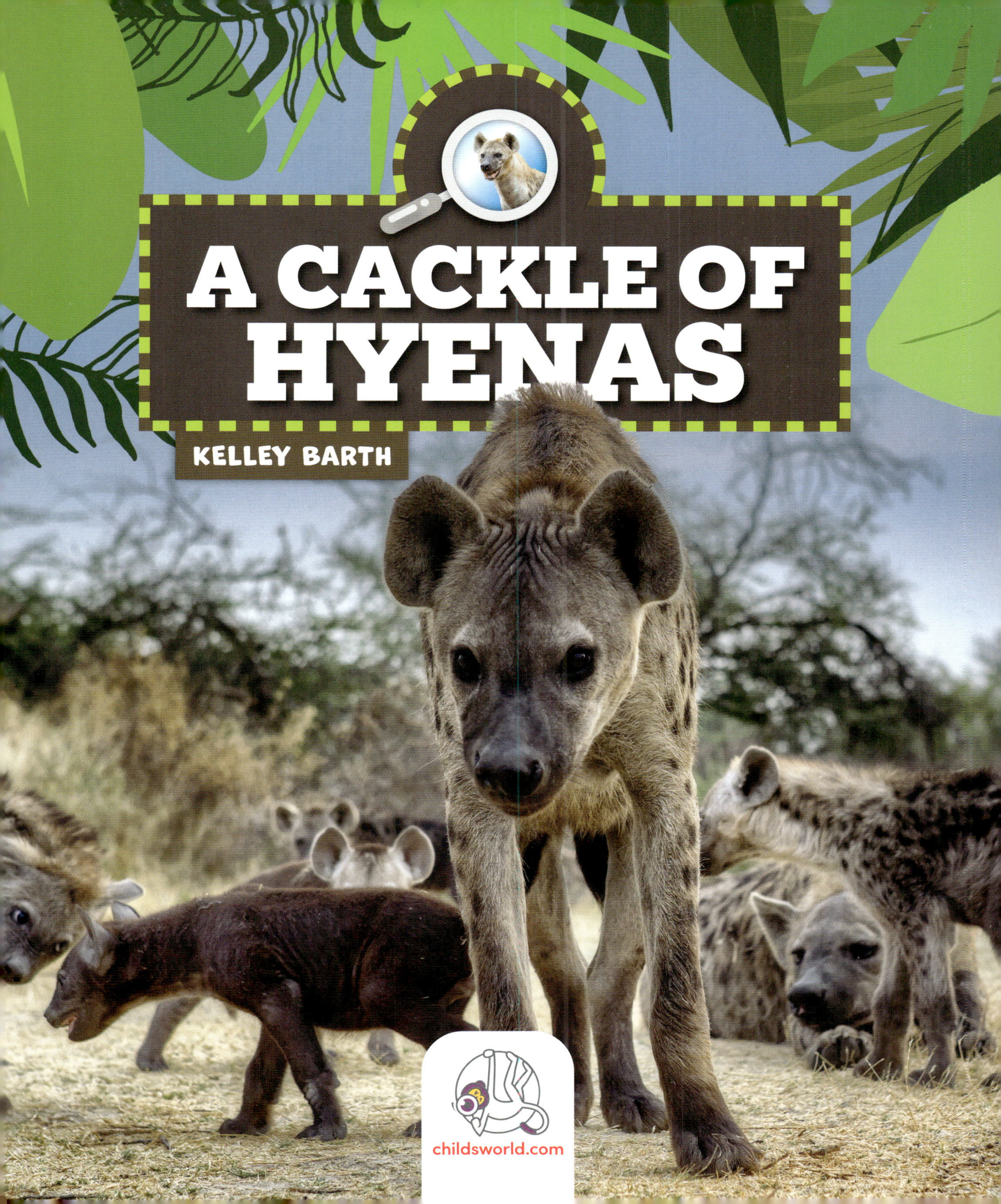
A CACKLE OF HYENAS
KELLEY BARTH
childsworld.com

Published by The Child's World®
800-599-READ • www.childsworld.com

Photography Credits
page 1: ©Deon De Villiers/Getty Images; page 1: ©AaronAmat/Getty Images; page 2: ©Anastasiia Verych/Shutterstock; page 5: ©Mint Images/Getty Images; page 6: ©guenterguni/Getty Images; page 10: ©vndrpttn/Getty Images; page 12: ©Londolozi Images/Mint Images/Getty Images; page 16: ©Manoj Shah/Getty Images; page 19: ©Robert Muckley/Getty Images; page 22: ©sumkinn/Shutterstock; page 22: ©Macrovector/Getty Images

ISBN Information
9781503885028 (Reinforced Library Binding)
9781503885844 (Portable Document Format)
9781503886483 (Online Multi-user eBook)
9781503887121 (Electronic Publication)

LCCN 2023937378

Printed in the United States of America

Kelley Barth is a former children's librarian who loves connecting with young people over stories and books. When she isn't busy writing, Kelley enjoys reading, hiking, crafting, and exploring national parks. She lives in Minnesota with her husband and dog.

TABLE OF CONTENTS

CHAPTER 1

Meet the Cackle

Dawn is breaking on the African **savanna**. A group of ten spotted hyenas watch the horizon for their next meal. Soon they spot a wildebeest. They're off! But this chase isn't about speed. The wildebeest might be faster, but hyenas can run long distances. The group will keep running until the wildebeest tires out and slows down. And when that happens, watch out! Hyenas have one of the strongest bites in the animal kingdom, and they are always hungry.

Hyenas look a lot like dogs, but they are really more similar to cats.

TYPES OF HYENAS

There are four different types of hyenas: aardwolves, brown hyenas, striped hyenas, and spotted hyenas. Striped and brown hyenas are the smallest hyenas. Spotted hyenas are the most social type and live in the biggest groups. They are also the most common. The other types of hyenas often hunt alone and live in much smaller groups.

The leader of the cackle stays on the lookout for hunting opportunities.

A group of hyenas is called a **cackle**. They are also sometimes called a clan or a pack. *Cackle* is another word for a loud laugh. Hyenas are well known for the laugh-like sound that they make. But hyenas are not actually laughing. The noises they make when they are excited or scared simply sound like laughter.

Cackles of spotted hyenas can be very large, with up to 130 members. Hyena cackles have a **hierarchy**. They have a very strict social order of who is in charge. This hierarchy helps hyena cackles work together and avoid fights.

Spotted hyena cackles live in Africa, south of the Sahara Desert. Cackles live in a number of different **habitats**. They live in woodlands, savannas, and semi-deserts. Many larger cackles live in protected areas, such as the Serengeti-Mara **ecosystem** and Kruger National Park in South Africa. Protected areas are pieces of land where animals cannot be hunted. Sometimes scientists study the animals that live in these areas.

A cackle works together to protect its **territory**. Small groups patrol its borders. These hyenas mark their scent to warn away other **predators** and competing cackles.

AFRICA
Atlantic Ocean
Indian Ocean
KEY
Where spotted hyenas live

CHAPTER 2

All in the Family

When they are ready to **mate**, female hyenas choose a partner. After about four months, the mother hyena will give birth. Baby hyenas are called cubs. Hyenas usually have between one and three cubs at a time. Mother hyenas take good care of their cubs. Before they give birth, the mother hyena will find a safe den separate from the rest of the cackle. She keeps her young cubs in this den for two weeks. The mother and cubs use this time to bond. The cubs even learn how to recognize their mother's voice.

Hyenas are good mothers and spend nearly all of their time caring for their newborn cubs.

Spotted hyenas are born with brown or black fur. They don't get their spots for a few months.

After two weeks, the mother hyena will bring her cubs to the cackle's large shared den. Here the cackle continues raising the cubs together. Cubs nurse on their mother's milk for more than a year while they grow up and learn about life in the cackle. Young cubs often play and fight with each other to prove their **dominance**.

Female hyenas stay in their cackles for life. After about two to three years, most male hyenas will leave their mother and join a new group.

Who's in Charge?

In hyena cackles, females are in charge. One female is the dominant leader of the group. Cubs gain their social status from their mother. Cubs of high-**ranking** mothers will also be high ranking. Cubs of lower-ranking mothers have a lower rank in the cackle hierarchy.

After they leave their mother's cackle, male hyenas join a new group at the bottom of the social hierarchy. Even newborn cubs outrank male hyenas in the cackle. The hierarchy of a cackle is very stable. When the leader dies, her oldest daughter usually takes over. It is rare for the hierarchy to break apart. But sometimes, low-ranking female hyenas leave to start a new cackle.

Spotted Hyena Size Comparison

Spotted hyenas are around 3–5 feet (.9–1.5 meters) long and 3.3 feet (1 m) tall. They weigh up to 180 pounds (82 kilograms).

The average house cat is 20-28 inches (51-71 centimeters) long and weighs between 8 and 12 pounds (3.6-5.5 kg).

Members of a cackle make funny faces at each other and bob their heads when they want to play or fight.

HYENAS VS. LIONS

Hyenas aren't the food thieves people often think they are. While a crafty hyena will sometimes steal a meal from another animal, lions steal far more food from hyenas. Spotted hyenas hunt for 60 to 90 percent of their food. However, scientists have found that as much as 80 percent of a lion's food is stolen from hyenas.

Cackle members have close bonds and work together to hunt large animals, defend their territory, and raise cubs. The cackle hierarchy also matters at mealtime. High-ranking females and their cubs get to eat first.

But living in a cackle isn't all work. Hyenas are very playful animals. Both cubs and adults play games, such as chase and keep-away. Hyenas are also strong swimmers and often splash or dunk each other for fun.

Cackles also do a good job communicating with each other. Hyenas groan, grunt, giggle, bark, and squeal to share information. A loud "whoop" lets other hyenas know that there is danger near, or that they need help.

What Makes the Cackle Unique?

Hyena cackles are unique in the animal world. Unlike most animals, female hyenas are larger and more aggressive than males. But a female hyena doesn't become the cackle leader just because of her size and strength. In the hyena world, power is all about who you know. A large social group is the most powerful tool a hyena can have. The more social support a female hyena has, the higher her ranking within the cackle. A high ranking is important. Higher-ranking female hyenas eat more food, live longer, and give birth to more cubs.

SCAVENGER HUNT

While spotted hyenas hunt together, brown and striped hyenas usually go looking for food alone. Since hunting without help from other hyenas is harder, striped and brown hyenas are more likely to snatch food from other big animals, such as lions. They tend to scavenge at night when darkness gives them an easy cover for theft. Striped and brown hyenas also look for meals in garbage cans or on the side of the road. Their scavenging ways put them at risk of attack from predators and humans.

Brown hyenas are also sometimes called strandwolves.

CHAPTER 5

Why Cackles Matter

Hyenas have often been considered mean, ugly scavengers. But hyenas are smart and highly social animals. Hyenas are also **keystone** predators. They keep their ecosystem healthy by hunting and eating weak prey. Hyenas get most of their food from hunting. But they aren't picky eaters. Hyenas also help their ecosystems by eating dead animals that other predators won't. Powerful jaws and strong stomachs help hyenas digest diseased animals and even large bones.

Cackles help hyenas protect themselves and have more success hunting. Living and working together as a group is part of what makes hyenas so special.

Wonder More

Wondering about New Information

What new information did you learn about hyena cackles? Write down three new facts that you learned. Did this information surprise you? Why or why not?

Wondering How It Matters

Cackles have a very strict hierarchy. How does this hierarchy help hyenas? What other animals or groups have a similar hierarchy?

Wondering Why

Why do you think living in a cackle is helpful to hyenas? Why are they important? Why do you think hyenas are often thought of as "bad" animals?

Ways to Keep Wondering

After reading this book, what questions do you have about hyena cackles? What can you do to learn more about them?

Hyena Family Tree

Hyenas have very strict social structures. Try creating your own hyena family tree to find out where each animal falls in the cackle hierarchy.

What You Need:

- paper
- pencil
- crayons, colored pencils, markers (optional)

Steps to Take:

1. Design and draw your hyena hierarchy. At the top of the chart make sure to have the highest-ranking female hyena. Directly underneath should be her offspring.

2. Follow this pattern down the chart with medium and lower ranking female hyenas and their pups.

3. Finally, at the bottom of your hierarchy should be the male hyenas who joined the cackle.

4. Label your hyenas and their rankings. Give each hyena a name and a unique design so you can tell them apart.

Glossary

cackle (KAK-ul) A cackle is a harsh or sharp laugh.

dominance (DOM-ih-nunss) Dominance is the state of being in control or having power in a social hierarchy.

ecosystem (EE-koh-sis-tem) An ecosystem is a community of living things and their environment functioning as a unit.

habitat (HAB-ih-tat) A habitat is the place where a plant or animal normally lives.

hierarchy (HY-ur-ar-kee) A hierarchy is a group organized into orders or ranks.

keystone (KEE-stohn) A keystone predator is an animal that helps bring balance an ecosystem.

mate (MAYT) When animals mate, they join together to produce offspring.

predator (PREH-duh-tuhr) A predator is an animal that hunts other animals for food.

ranking (RANK-ing) Ranking is an animal or person's place in a hierarchy.

savanna (suh-VAN-uh) A savanna is a large grassland with few trees.

territory (TAYR-ih-tor-ee) Territory is the physical area that an animal or group lives on or defends.

Find Out More

In the Library

Corrigan, Sophie. *The Not Bad Animals.* Minneapolis, MN: Frances Lincoln Children's Books, 2020.

Levy, Janet. *Hyenas Bite!* New York, NY: Gareth Stevens Publishing, 2021.

Sommer, Nathan. *Animal Battles: Lion vs. Hyena Clan.* Minneapolis, MN: Bellwether Media, 2020.

On the Web

Visit our website for links about hyena cackles:
childsworld.com/links

Note to Parents, Caregivers, Teachers, and Librarians: We routinely verify our web links to make sure they are safe and active sites. So encourage your readers to check them out!

Index